Shipwrecks
of North Devon

Richard and Bridget Larn

Tor Mark Press • Redruth

Other Devonshire titles in the Tor Mark Series

Birds of Devon
Classic Devon ghost stories
Clotted cream
Devon customs and superstitions
Devonshire jokes and stories
Devon legends
Wild flowers of the Devon coast

Other shipwreck titles in the Tor Mark series

Shipwrecks around Land's End
Shipwrecks around the Lizard
Shipwrecks around Mount's Bay
Shipwrecks on Cornwall's North coast
Shipwrecks – Falmouth to Looe
Tales of the Cornish wreckers

First published 1999 by Tor Mark Press
PO Box 4, Redruth, Cornwall TR16 5YX

ISBN 0-85025-381-0

© 1999 Tor Mark Press
All rights reserved

Acknowledgements

Acknowledgement is gratefully given to the many early photographers of shipwrecks in Devon and Cornwall, as well as many collectors, who have made this book possible. In particular we want to acknowledge and thank the following: R L Knight Ltd of Barnstaple; A Headon of Bideford; G Reilly, North Devon; A Matthews, Clovelly; Gibson Kyne, Isles of Scilly; *Western Morning News*; the Hawkes of Helston; the late E Collins of Penzance; and Joshua Behenna of Slapton, South Devon.

Printed in Great Britain by Cornwall Litho, Redruth

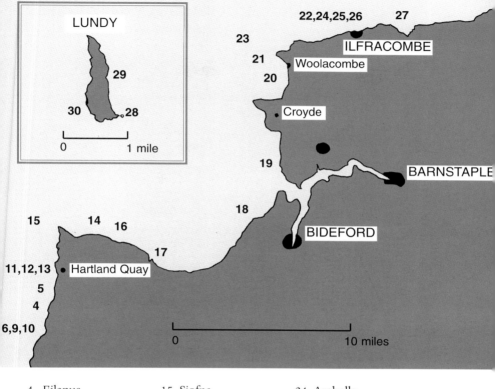

4 Eilanus	15 Sjofna	24 Arabella
5 Katina	16 Abril	25 Marie Emilie
6 Goliath	17 Harlseywood	26 Nikita
9 Green Ranger	18 Madeleine	27 Aberlemno
10 Flora	19 Fimmo	28 Carmine Filomena
11 Rosalia	20 A.C.L.	29 Maria Kyriakides
12 Cingetorix	21 Newtown	30 Montagu
13 Johanna	22 Moewe	
14 Huddersfield	23 Dido C	

The coasts of North Devon and Lundy hold over ten wrecks for every mile, but unfortunately few were photographed. Although larger ships would normally give Hartland and Lundy a wide berth when heading for or leaving Bristol or the coal ports of South Wales, fog was their biggest enemy. In bad weather, smaller craft could only seek the lee of Lundy, or attempt to reach Bideford or Barnstaple, since this coast has not even one deep water port.

Above: Built as the SS *Wyke Regis*, later renamed the *Eilanus* and registered at Liverpool, this ship was carrying 800 tons of scrap metal from Le Havre to Briton Ferry when she went ashore in dense fog at night at Welcombe Mouth on 16 June 1936. Her eleven man crew took to the boats and drifted around all night, landing at daybreak.

Opposite: The Greek steamship *Katina*, of 2899 tons gross, went ashore on a high spring tide beneath the Elmscott Cliffs in fog during the night of 23 May 1913, whilst in ballast bound from Athens to Barry Docks. Her crew got ashore and climbed the 120 metre high cliffs. She was later pulled off by the tug *Etna*, then repaired at Clovelly, where she is seen in the lower photograph opposite.

S.S. KATINA. BEACHED AT CLOVELLY. JUNE. 7. 13
STRANDED OFF HARTLAND. 23 MAY. 13.

5

A French fishing trawler of Lorient, the *Goliath*, stranded under
Sandor Cliffs, Knap Head, on 16 March 1969, half a mile from
where the RFA *Green Ranger* had been lost seven years earlier. No
one on shore knew of the accident until two bedraggled French
seamen appeared in the doorway of Elmscott Farm at 7am.
Finding her abandoned, modern day 'wreckers' stripped her of
valuable equipment which the police and customs had to retrieve.
Within three weeks the *Goliath* was smashed to pieces.

The Royal Fleet Auxiliary tanker *Green Ranger* was under tow of the tug *Caswell* from Devonport to Cardiff for a refit when she broke adrift in a force 10 gale during the afternoon of 17 November 1962 and drifted ashore under the high cliffs at Longpeak. The crew were saved in a gallant rescue involving both the Clovelly lifeboat and the Hartland LSA breeches buoy.

Above: In ballast from Genoa to Newport to load coal, the Italian
SS *Rosalia*, built in 1892 as the *Polana*, made such a large hole in her
hull when she went ashore in dense fog close to the old coastguard
station at Hartland Quay on 27 May 1905, that she became a total
wreck, close to what is now the Hartland Museum.

Opposite: Her name and port of registry painted in large letters
to denote her neutrality during the First World War, the Dutch
steamer *Flora* was wrecked in fog under the 60 metre high cliffs of
Longpeak, two miles south of Hartland Point, on 6 April 1915. Her
crew remained on board until low water, when they were able to
walk ashore safely.

WRECK OF THE S.S CINGETORIX OFF HARTLAND

Above: When thick fog and a heavy ground swell set in during the night of 2 March 1911, a member of the local LSA crew was put on watch at Hartland Quay. He had no sooner reached his post than a ship's siren was heard close at hand, followed by distress rockets and, after climbing down 30 metre rope ladders, the team found the Belgian SS *Cingetorix* ashore, carrying a cargo of steel.

Opposite: After a career lasting 24 years, during which this motor vessel bore four different names, commencing with *Jurhil*, then *Heinrich Brand*, followed by *Elisa Johanna* and finally just *Johanna*, she went ashore in fog and heavy weather only 400 metres clear of Hartland Point lighthouse on New Year's Eve 1982. Gales quickly reduced the wreck to scrap steel, but before she broke up she was plundered of anything of value.

Above: The armed Norwegian SS *Sjofna* went ashore near Hartland Point carrying a cargo of china clay in bags from Fowey to Larne on 23 November 1944. Seven crew were saved by lifeboat, the other ten by breeches buoy. The second rocket fired from the cliffs went through the wheelhouse window, breaking the captain's right leg and setting fire to the ship's cat – which luckily survived!

Opposite: Another victim of fog, the SS *Huddersfield* of Cardiff, carrying coal from Barry Docks to Santa Elena, went ashore in a gale during the early hours of 27 January 1908 near Shipload Bay, Hartland. Nine crew took to a boat and rowed to Clovelly to raise the alarm. The Clovelly lifeboat then saved the remaining twelve left on board.

Above: This Middlesborough registered steamship, the *Harlseywood* of 2701 tons gross, was on passage from Penarth to St Nazaire carrying coal when she was torpedoed in the Bristol Channel on 17 July 1918. Captain Scott beached her at Widemouth, and she was then towed to Clovelly and beached again for repairs.

Opposite: Built in 1897 as the *Ardgour* at Campbeltown, later renamed *Abril*, and on passage from Newport to Bilbao with coal, this Spanish steamship went ashore in Beckland Bay, near Chapman Rock, on 16 February 1906. Sixteen crew reached Clovelly in one of her boats; another carrying four men drifted away on the tide but was later found by the Clovelly lifeboat.

Having lost nearly all her sails in a gale in Bideford Bay whilst
homeward bound for Fécamp from Swansea with coal, the French
schooner *Madeleine* went ashore at Westward Ho! during the night
of 31 August 1908. She was later refloated and repaired at
Appledore. Her five man crew scrambled over her bow and got
ashore, spending the remainder of the night on Northam Burrows,
unaware of their location. No one on shore had seen the wreck.

This German auxiliary, steel, three-masted schooner, the *Fimmo*, built at Boitzenburg in 1917, was going over the bar of the River Taw when one of her steering chains parted and she became unmanageable, unable to answer her rudder. She went ashore off Braunton, where the Appledore lifeboat took off her crew of nine. She was eventually refloated and repaired at Appledore, and in 1934 was sold and renamed *Fortunato Pio*, being sunk by air attack off Benghazi during the Second World War on 21 July 1940.

Above: Distress flares off Woolacombe on 7 January 1916 alerted the coast watcher in charge of the rocket apparatus at Mortehoe that a vessel was ashore. This proved to be the London steamer *Newtown*, 1153 tons gross, carrying pit props to Newport. She went ashore in fog and was left perched high and dry near Harris's Cove. Her captain, the last of the 19 crew to leave, was drowned when washed out of the breeches buoy. She became a total loss.

Opposite: This French brig with the unusual name of *A.C.L.* registered at Nantes, which had artificial gunports painted on both sides, ran ashore on Woolacombe Sands in dense fog on 25 January 1894. She was bound to Cardiff from Bordeaux in ballast. Her six man crew were brought ashore by breeches buoy. She is shown here beached in Ilfracombe Harbour with a broken main topmast and other damage, awaiting repair.

Above: The Barnstaple wooden fishing ketch *Dido C* got on the Morte Stone, off Morte Point, on a falling tide, and at low water was left in this dangerous and precarious position. Fortunately she suffered no damage and on the next high water was successfully refloated and saved.

Opposite: The 339 ton German barque *Moewe* sank following collision with the full-rigged ship *Celtic Chief*, of Liverpool, off Bull Point near Mortehoe on 19 June 1888. The *Moewe* was later raised and taken into Ilfracombe Harbour, and the photograph shows her being broken up.

The Arabella, *apparently safe in Ilfracombe Harbour (above), but actually high and dry (below)*

Above: Spectators crowd the pierhead at Ilfracombe to watch salvage operations being carried out on the Barnstaple registered ketch *Marie Emilie.* Carrying coal from Newport to Barnstaple, she got on the rocks on 18 October 1886. Her crew of two managed to reach the shore safely, but after being refloated the wooden vessel was found to be damaged beyond repair and was broken up at Ilfracombe.

Opposite: The wooden ketch *Arabella*, of Gloucester, built in the River Severn at the village of Saul in 1864, was left perched high and dry on Britton Rock, at the southern entrance of Ilfracombe Harbour and became a total wreck on 2 October 1895. Her crew of four and two local men on board at the time were all drowned. The high cliffs surrounding the harbour frequently caused sailing vessels to go ashore.

Above: Following an offshore collision in the Bristol Channel with another sailing vessel, the wooden schooner *Nikita*, shown on her beam ends on the left of this photograph, managed to reach Ilfracombe Harbour in September 1894 before sinking.

Opposite: The iron barque *Aberlemno* of Swansea, bound from Burry Port to Rio de Janeiro with 1400 tons of coal, got off course in a snowstorm and went ashore on Egg Rock, near Watermouth Cove, on 2 April 1897. The Ilfracombe lifeboat went to her assistance in dreadful weather conditions, and with the help of men from Combe Martin who had managed to get on board, laid out a kedge anchor by which means she was refloated using only the ship's windlass. She was then taken into Ilfracombe and allowed to dry out in the harbour so that several small leaks could be cured, after which she continued her voyage. Built at Dumbarton in 1876, she was finally broken up in 1924 when under the Swedish flag.

Above: One of the few wrecks to take place on the east side of Lundy was the Greek SS *Maria Kyriakides*, which went ashore on Quarry Beach under the old hospital on 24 March 1929, her crew of fourteen being saved. She remained ashore for almost a year before being refloated and towed to Ilfracombe where her cargo was discharged. Too badly damaged for repair, she was broken up at Newport.

Opposite: The Italian steamship *Carmine Filomena*, registered at Genoa and carrying a cargo of coal from Swansea to her home port, stranded on Mouse Island, at the extreme south-east corner of Lundy Island, on 1 July 1937 in fog. She became a total wreck.

The total loss of the battleship HMS *Montagu* when she was wrecked on Lundy on 30 May 1906 was a serious blow to the Royal Navy. Engaged in early wireless experiments out of Milford Haven, she became enveloped in dense fog whilst at anchor. Given the very real danger of collision with merchant vessels, she was moved closer inshore where she struck Shutter Rock and sank. A landing party scaled the cliffs and walked the full length of Lundy to the north lighthouse where an argument ensued with the keeper, the lieutenant from the ship insisting it was Hartland Point light!

Despite every attempt by her crew to seal the holes and pump her dry, followed by every available assistance from the Naval Dockyard at Milford Haven, she was declared a total loss. Her four 12 inch main gun barrels were removed and towed back to the dockyard on lighters, after which Captain Young of the Liverpool Salvage Association recovered other guns, stores and fittings, then the Western Marine Salvage Company of Penzance broke up the wreck for scrap metal.

After the first few days *(above)* access to the wreck was gained by means of an overhead walkway supported by steel cables from the shore attached to the foremast, enabling the salvage workers to dispense with the need for boats.

Literally hundreds of dockyard workers, in addition to her 750 man crew, were involved in attempting to salvage the 14,000 ton warship, which had been built at Devonport Dockyard in 1901.

Failure to save the ship was due to the fact that Admiral Sir A K Wilson RN was put in charge, having no salvage experience, and by the time Captain Young was appointed in his place the underwater damage was too great for even this experienced civilian salvage officer.